XTREME

acoustic
guitar

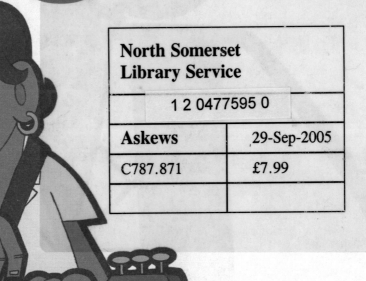

Andrew Ellis

smt

acoustic guitar

CV
NL
WL

Ple

ACKNOWLEDGEMENTS

Many, many thanks to:

All my family and friends. Bruce, Damien, Jon and everyone at the Brighton Institute of Modern Music. Abbo (Research assistance and toast advice). Tim Davies (Photography and amusing attempts at voice of Frett). Paul Ellis (Widdle FX). Gavin Fitzpatrick (Modelling).Carlos Garcia (Voice of Frett). Dan Partington (Clapping and bald-head percussion). Rachael Wood (Modelling, proofreading, widdle FX, clapping... and coffee). Jarry Hughes.

www.AREmusic.co.uk

Printed in the United Kingdom by
MPG Books Ltd, Bodmin

Published by SMT, an imprint of
Sanctuary Publishing Limited
Sanctuary House
45–53 Sinclair Road
London W14 0NS
United Kingdom

www.sanctuarypublishing.com

ISBN: 1-84492-039-9

CONTENTS

INTRODUCTION

Welcome to *Xtreme Acoustic Guitar*. This is your introduction to the instrument that gets just about everywhere: Granny keeps a dusty one in the attic, the busker dude down the subway is always strumming one... oh, and all those stars performing to crowds of thousands – they've got one or two!

We've got a great mix of lessons, artist stories and style examples to get you up and running, all backed up with a CD to strum along to. There'll be plenty of fun and we might sneak in some important theory stuff when you're not looking!

MEET YOUR TUTOR

So, let's introduce Frett, your tutor throughout this book. It has proved impossible to find a photograph of Frett without his guitar (apart from the one as a baby in the bath), so you can guarantee he's the man to show you the way. He'll explain how the acoustic guitar works and teach you the essential skills to practise – just make sure he doesn't go on too much about his travelling adventures!

FRETT IS HERE TO GUIDE YOU...

'Hello my friends! It's nice to meet you. I hope you're as excited as I am. There's nothing better than reminiscing over the times I've had with my guitar.

Now, the acoustic guitar is a mean songwriting machine, and you'll find it in many styles of music. We'll go through some lessons to teach the basic skills that will leave you fit to set off in whatever direction you like.'

ADVISE YOU...

'Oh, I could tell you some stories. I've spent most of my life travelling the world with this guitar, met a lot of people and heard a lot of sounds. You know it can be great to find some guitar idols to influence your playing and keep you keen.

We'll find out who the main strummers are and how they made their names in the music industry. We'll also look at how they do what they do and have a go at playing along in their styles. Be sure to have a listen – you are what you eat!'

TEST YOU...

'Tests?! Essays?! Exams?! Nah, don't you worry, it's nothing scary. The guitar is fun, not a punishment. If you get stuck you can always listen to the CD or read the lessons again. I just want to make sure you're doing OK or else it's gonna make me look bad!'

MAKE YOU LAUGH...!

'They say a dog is man's best friend. Well, for me it's my guitar! There are no bad smells, and it doesn't eat that much, apart from the occasional plectrum and pack of strings. Now where's your guitar, huh? Go fetch!'

YOUR ACOUSTIC GUITAR

Let me introduce my guitar. It's a tasty one, yeah? I know the patterns in its wood like the back of my hand.

SOUNDHOLE The soundhole is not just there to lose your plectrum in! This is where the sound comes out for us to hear.

SOUNDBOX The hollow inside of the acoustic guitar is referred to as the soundbox or 'acoustic chamber'. Without this space the strings wouldn't sound very loud at all. The shape of it determines the volume and quality of sound.

SOUNDBOARD The front of the guitar body is called the soundboard. When you strum the strings loudly you'll feel the wood vibrating.

BRIDGE This is where the strings attach to the body of the guitar. The bridge sets the height and length of the strings. The strings send vibrations through the bridge to the soundboard and then into the soundbox. How the strings attach to the bridge can depend on your guitar. A steel-string guitar will either have bridge pins that trap the string ball ends into holes or a slotted bridge that you thread the strings through. Nylon-string guitars don't have ball ends on their strings so you loop and tie them to the bridge.

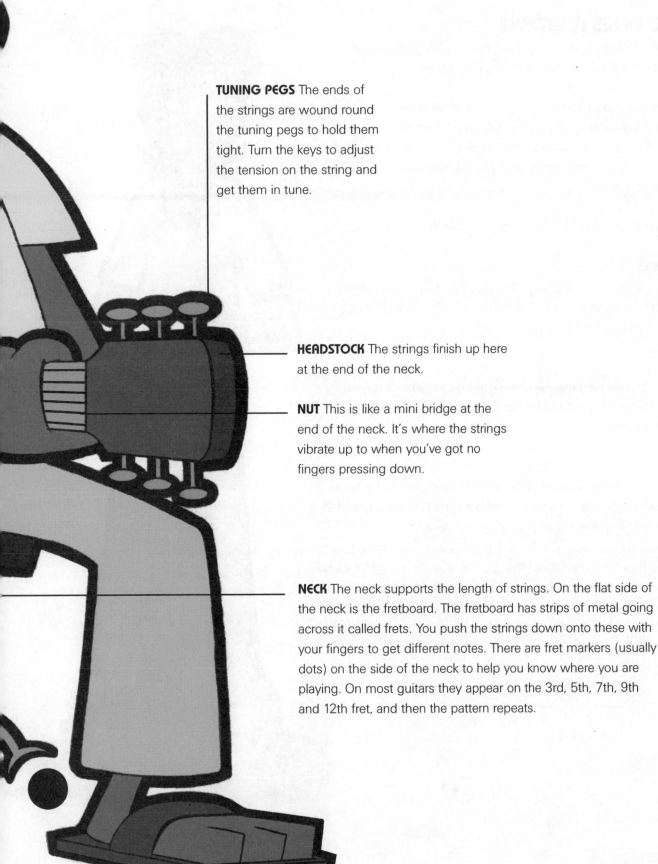

TUNING PEGS The ends of the strings are wound round the tuning pegs to hold them tight. Turn the keys to adjust the tension on the string and get them in tune.

HEADSTOCK The strings finish up here at the end of the neck.

NUT This is like a mini bridge at the end of the neck. It's where the strings vibrate up to when you've got no fingers pressing down.

NECK The neck supports the length of strings. On the flat side of the neck is the fretboard. The fretboard has strips of metal going across it called frets. You push the strings down onto these with your fingers to get different notes. There are fret markers (usually dots) on the side of the neck to help you know where you are playing. On most guitars they appear on the 3rd, 5th, 7th, 9th and 12th fret, and then the pattern repeats.

WOODEN YOU LIKE TO KNOW!

CD TRACK 2

HOW DOES IT WORK?

We'll check out how to tune up later, but the CD contains a set of reference notes so you can play along with my examples.

It's handy to understand why us guitarists do what we do. Have you ever tried 'boinging' a ruler on the edge of a table? The note of the 'boing' changes as you shorten the length of the ruler over the edge. Plucking a string is just the same. It's the vibrating length of string that we hear as a note.

There are three things that affect the note that the string makes:

THICKNESS

The thicker the string, the lower the note. You may have spotted that there are six strings, starting with a really thick one, and then getting gradually thinner.

TENSION

The tuning pegs hold the strings tight along the guitar. A tighter string vibrates faster and so we hear a higher note. This is how we tune the strings.

LENGTH

A shorter string also vibrates faster and so, again, we hear a higher note. Pushing the strings onto the fretboard shortens the length that vibrates and therefore raises the pitch of the note.

So that's how we make music! The acoustic guitar is a magical thing: no batteries and no wires, but lots of noise. Well, it's not magic really. The strings make the wood shake and, in turn, all the sound vibrates through the air inside the guitar, out of the soundhole and off to our ears. Clever stuff.

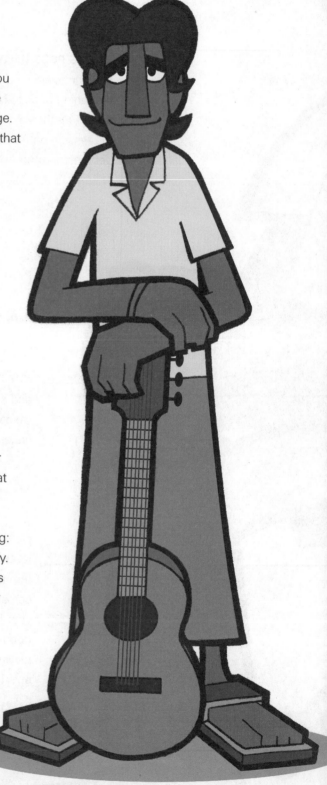

READING TABLATURE

Guitar Tablature, or TAB, is the simplest way to notate guitar music and you'll stumble across it throughout this book. You've done painting by numbers? Well, this is kind of like guitar playing by numbers.

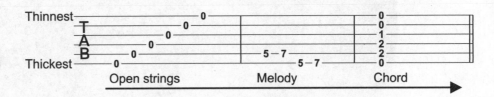

| Thinnest | | Open strings | Melody | Chord | Thickest |

The strings are laid out horizontally, starting from the bottom to the top, from the thickest to the thinnest. The numbers refer to the fret space and string to put your finger on and pluck.

Read across the chart from left to right, just as you're reading this book, and, as you encounter a number, play it! If you come across numbers in a vertical line, play all those strings at once.

You can compare what you're playing to my examples on the CD if you're not sure.

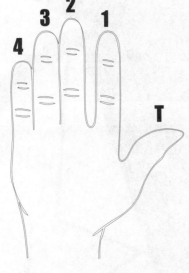

HANDS

To make sure that both the right- and left-handed folk out there understand what I'm talking about:

'FRET' HAND The one holding the neck, pushing the strings onto the frets.
'PICK' HAND The one over the body, plucking the strings.

Some of the lessons require you to use specific fingers of your fret hand. Here's a hand diagram showing the numbers that we use – your index finger is number 1, and so on.

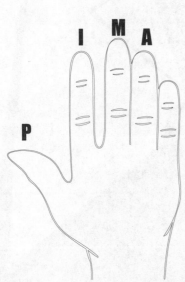

Likewise, when playing fingerstyle, I'll need to show you when to pluck with your thumb or fingers. This hand diagram indicates the letters that we use. 'Why PIMA?' I knew you'd ask that! It's Spanish:

'PULGAR' = THUMB, 'INDICE' = FOREFINGER, 'MEDIO' = MIDDLE FINGER, 'ANULAR' = RING FINGER.

LESSONS

GET COMFORTABLE

Hey you! Ready to twang those strings? This first lesson is all about getting to know the guitar and giving your fingers a taste of what's lying ahead. Things might seem strange to start with but some regular practice will help you feel at home with the old wood and strings.

YOUR GOALS

GOAL 1
To hold the guitar correctly when sitting down and standing up.

GOAL 2
To get your hands in the correct positions.

GOAL 3
To experiment with different picking techniques.

GOAL 4
To make some noise!

THEORY

Have a look at the photos to see the position of the guitar, arms, hands, fingers and thumbs. All these bits need to come together to make a good playing style. Your choice of acoustic guitar is also quite important as they come in different shapes and sizes. If you're going shopping, make sure it fits!

Standard playing position when seated

Standard playing position when standing

IN PRACTICE

Let's grab our six-string and get into position.

STEP 1

Always try to keep your back straight. When sitting down, rest the guitar body on your right leg (left-handers on your left leg). Or, if you fancy the classical approach, try with the guitar body sat between your legs. This brings the neck angle up higher – you might need a footstool so you're not too hunched up. Just find a position that doesn't leave you feeling tense and you'll have got it about right.

STEP 2

When standing up, try to get the strap height so the guitar is in roughly the same position as when you are sitting – that way you won't feel too lost when you need to walk around on stage.

STEP 3

The fret hand's job is to push the strings down against the metal frets, with the fingertip just above them. Get your fingers and thumb roughly parallel to the frets and squeeze with your thumb behind the neck. Imagine you've got your hand in a glove puppet that's trying to take a bite out of the neck!

STEP 4

Your fret elbow shouldn't be tucked into your body, nor should it be stuck out like a chicken wing – somewhere in-between. Check the photos (see p15).

STEP 5

The pick hand is for getting the strings to vibrate and there are a few choices on technique. The thumb and/or fingers can strum up and down the strings or pluck them individually with fingernails or flesh. Alternatively you can use a 'plectrum' or 'pick'. Hold the pick between the first finger and thumb and hit the strings with the pointy end. Big strums should come from twisting your wrist and bending your elbow. Smaller, single-string picks come from your fingers, thumb and, again, the twisting wrist.

The following lessons will look at all this in more detail.

PROBLEM?

If it hurts, stop! Stretch out or take a rest. These are new movements to your fingers, wrists and arms. Your fingertips on both hands will get sore but, after a few weeks, they'll build up a tougher layer of skin to deal with the new activity.

EXERCISE

Right, let's see what you've got. I've learned loads of stuff just by randomly plonking my fingers onto the strings and seeing what happens. Check me messing about on the CD track and give it a go for yourself. Experiment and see what you like!

1. You can strum all the strings at once with your thumb, a plectrum or fingers. Try strumming up and down the strings. For the moment, don't worry too much about getting nice sounds, and ignore anybody who's giving you funny looks!

2. Pluck individual strings in different combinations. Again, you have a choice of thumb, fingers, plectrum or a mixture!

3. Hit the strings hard or pluck them softly. Get some percussive sounds and stop notes ringing by resting either hand lightly over the strings.

4. Make use of all four fingers on the fretboard. You'll probably have one finger that's particularly badly behaved. Keep trying – it'll get the message sooner or later.

TIP

We've now seen that the picking hand has a lot of different techniques to choose from. Give each method a try in the exercises that we work on. A particular technique may feel more natural, and it's ok to concentrate a little more on that. Most artists will favour the one picking technique, which is what gives them their distinct sounds.

TEST

QUESTION 1

Which hand is your picking hand?

QUESTION 2

Why do we have different picking techniques to choose from?

QUESTION 3

What should you do if things start to hurt?

QUESTION 4

Why should your strap height be set up to match the guitar's sitting position?

TUNE UP

'What? You need tuning? OK, I'll be there in a minute…' So, I talk to my guitar – so what? Anyway, this section is the key to making everything sound great. If the guitar strings aren't tuned properly, your audience ain't gonna stick around for long!

YOUR GOALS

GOAL 1
To understand the musical alphabet.

GOAL 2
To remember the notes that each string is tuned to.

GOAL 3
To train your ears to recognise the difference between two notes.

GOAL 4
To get the guitar in tune.

THEORY

We'll be encountering letters to describe the different notes and chords, so, let's first get an idea of what that's all about. Musical notes are given letters of the alphabet. The good news is that they don't go all the way up to Z. They go from A to G and then start again. The weird bit is that there are notes in-between called 'sharps' or 'flats'. A sharp note has the '♯' symbol after it, a flat note has a '♭' symbol. This tends to make more sense to pianists but us strummers need to have a grasp too: Notice that there isn't a sharp/flat note from B to C and E to F. Memorise that and you're well on your way.

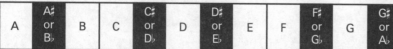

A	A♯ or B♭	B	C	C♯ or D♭	D	D♯ or E♭	E	F	F♯ or G♭	G	G♯ or A♭

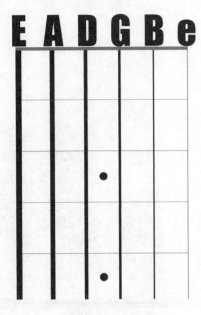

E A D G B e

Now we'll have a look at which of these notes the strings are tuned to. The standard tuning is shown to the left.

To help yourself remember, use a phrase such as:

Every **A**ngry **D**og **G**rowls **B**efore **E**ating

So now I should be able to say, 'Play the D string' and you'll know what to do. Also, I hope you've noticed we've got two E strings. We call the thicker string with the lower pitch 'low E' and the thin string with the higher pitch (two octaves higher) 'high E'.

Tuning up is going to involve training your ears to recognise if two notes sound the same. When their pitches are far apart it should be reasonably obvious. When they are the same they should almost sound like one. If the two notes are very similar you might hear a pulsing sound as they interfere with each other – these pulses are known as 'beats'. Listen for this effect to tell you that the strings are nearly in tune. If a note is tuned too high we say that it is 'sharp' and if it's too low we say that it is 'flat'.

IN PRACTICE

We're going to learn to tune up with a technique called 'relative tuning'. One string is tuned by listening to a reference note, perhaps from a piano. With that string correct, you tune the other strings from it. Have a go:

STEP 1

Listen to the tuning track on the CD (Track 2) to hear what the low E string should sound like (or play another instrument's E). Play your low E string and adjust its tuning peg until they sound the same. This is now your reference note on the guitar.

STEP 2

So, how do we know what the A string should sound like? Well, if you put a finger on the fifth fret of the E string that we just tuned, it will give the note A. Therefore, play that to hear the note we're aiming for and then play the A string to hear the difference. Adjust the A string tuning peg until it sounds the same.

STEP 3

Now that the A string is in tune we can use it to tune the D string. This time play the fifth fret of the A string and it will give us a D. You guessed it – tune the D string to this.

STEP 4

Next, the G string can be tuned to the fifth fret of the D string.

STEP 5

Now that you're getting used to this pattern, it's time to be awkward. With the G string now in tune, we use it as our reference to tune the B string, but this note is on the fourth fret of the G string (not the fifth like we have been doing).

STEP 6

For the final high E string, we go back to the old formula of playing the fifth fret of the B string to give us the note E. Nice one!

To check that all went well, it's best to give your favourite chord a strum and see if it sounds sweet (we'll come to chords later). If it makes you pull a face, go through the steps again to fine-tune everything.

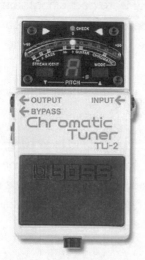

TIP

When you need to tune quickly, it's best to use an electronic tuner. Make sure the tuner has a microphone to pick up the sound of your acoustic. If your guitar has an electric pickup fitted, plug it directly into the box. A needle or light indicates the note and whether it's sharp, flat or in tune. Try not to neglect the fifth-fret method though, as you don't want to be dependent on a little box of tricks.

Above are a couple of examples of electronic tuners

EXERCISE

1. Below is the fifth-fret tuning method written out in tablature. This is demonstrated on the CD. Listen out for the open strings that initially sound out of tune and then get adjusted to match the reference note.

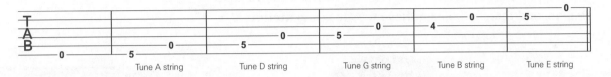

Tune A string   Tune D string   Tune G string   Tune B string   Tune E string

TRACK 5 CD

2. You can also use the tuning track on the CD to tune up all the strings as I play through them:

TRACK 6 CD

PROBLEM?

When learning the music of some acoustic guitarists, it may seem that they have extremely long and bendy fingers to get the tunes you hear. Well, they often use different tunings from the standard EADGBe such as DADGAd. This gives access to different sounds. To avoid getting freaked out, we'll only concentrate on the standard tuning, but bear it in mind. Songs may appear extremely tricky until you know the secret formula!

TEST

QUESTION 1
What phrase can you use to remember the string tunings?

QUESTION 2
Which string do we tune with the fourth fret of the previous string?

QUESTION 3
Which notes have no sharp/flat note between them?

EAR TRAINING I'll play ten pairs of notes on the CD. See if you can work out if the second note of each pair is sharp, flat or in tune. If you've got a music buddy, test each other with your own choice of notes.

TRACK 7 CD

FINGERSTYLE 1

You again? Cool! In this lesson we're going to look at fingerstyle.
This involves plucking individual strings with the thumb and
fingers, and then combining these moves into patterns.

YOUR GOALS

GOAL 1
To pluck the strings
accurately with the
thumb and fingers.

GOAL 2
To move fingers
independently of
each other.

GOAL 3
To learn some picking
patterns.

GOAL 4
To strengthen your
finger wave!

THEORY

The method we'll follow is to have the thumb (P) handling the three bass strings – low E, A and D. The remaining strings have a finger each, so that's the index finger (I) on the G string, middle finger (M) on the B string and ring finger (A) on the high E string. We'll use this fingerstyle routine throughout the book.

Check the photos to see how the hand should be positioned. Note how the three fingers are lined up above their allocated strings, while the thumb has the three bass strings all within reach.

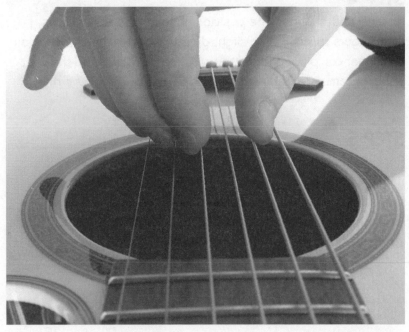

Try to have your hand hovering above the strings with no contact made on the guitar body. With this approach there is no restriction in motion.

IN PRACTICE

Get your plucking fingers on their marks.

STEP 1

Before playing, make sure that you're warmed up. Wiggle the fingers. Stretch out the arms and wrists.

STEP 2

Rest your fingertips on their allocated strings and your thumb on the low E string. Start with your fingers straight so they're standing tall on the strings. Now relax this a little so your fingers bend into more of a claw. Your wrist should be floating up off the guitar, as in the photos (see p23).

STEP 3

Start by plucking with the thumb. Push against and through the string so that it bends slightly and then quickly flicks off the edge of the thumb to sound a note. Your thumb can either finish the stroke up towards the palm of your hand or follow through and rest silently on to the next string. Each stroke has a slightly different sound.

STEP 4

Now try with a finger. The position of your hand should cause your fingers to move on a slight diagonal across the string. Again, the finger can pluck and curl towards the palm to avoid the next string or remain slightly straighter and rest on the next string.

STEP 5

Repeat with each finger. The little finger can get involved if you like, although we won't be making any use of it through the examples in this book. Sorry little finger! Get a feel for where the strings are and practise, ensuring only the intended string sounds.

PROBLEM?

The floating hand position may not feel completely natural at first but is worth persevering with. However, I'm not going to be too strict, just as long as you sound cool – this is Xtreme acoustic guitar after all! You'll come across slightly different fingerstyle techniques depending on the style you study, and who you talk to. Variations include stabilising your hand with your little finger anchored onto the soundboard, or resting the heel of your hand on the bridge just below the strings.

EXERCISE

These exercises all use open strings to concentrate on your picking hand. The other one will get its turn soon, though, so keep it handy!

1. We'll start off by going through each string, plucking it four times. The fingers to use are indicated above the TAB.

Try playing the first note of each group a bit louder than the other three. Count along with each pick – '1, 2, 3, 4, 1, 2, 3, 4, etc' and emphasise the 1s. At the start and end of this example you'll see double barlines with two dots. These are repeat marks and basically mean when you get to the end, start again.

TRACK 8

2 & 3. We'll now try two patterns that alternate between the thumb and fingers.

TRACKS 9 & 10

4 & 5. Here all fingers are involved one after the other, a bit like if you're drumming impatiently on a desk.

TRACKS 11 & 12

6. As you become familiar with these exercises, try to get your fingers plucking at the same volume and work on an even timing between notes.

TRACKS 11 & 12

> ### TIP
> Some guitarists will grow and shape their nails to pick with. This can help with accuracy, speed and give a brighter sound. A similar approach is to wear thumb and finger picks. Alternatively you can use your fingertips for a bit more feel and a mellower sound.

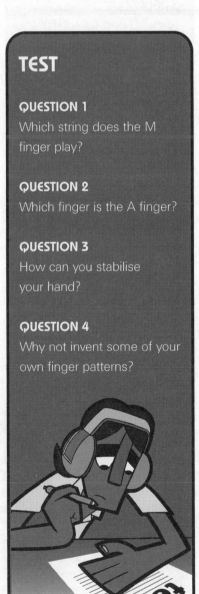

TEST

QUESTION 1
Which string does the M finger play?

QUESTION 2
Which finger is the A finger?

QUESTION 3
How can you stabilise your hand?

QUESTION 4
Why not invent some of your own finger patterns?

FRETTING

Got a sore neck looking down at your picking hand? Well let's turn our attentions to the fret hand. This is where all the extra notes and chords can come from.

THEORY

To fret a note, your fingertip should push the string down towards the fretboard so that it makes contact with the metal fret. Keep your thumb behind the neck so you've got something to press against.

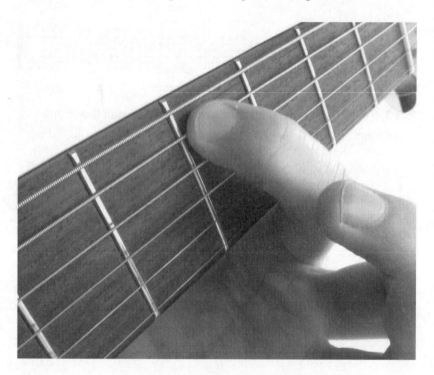

The ideal position for your finger is just before the fret wire. If the finger is too far away, the note will buzz. If the finger is too close, it will stop the string vibrating below the fret and you won't hear very much at all.

IN PRACTICE

It's time to venture out onto the fretboard, my friends.

STEP 1

As with fingerstyle, make sure that your fret fingers are warm and ready to start the exercises. You don't want to end up with a finger limp now, do you?!

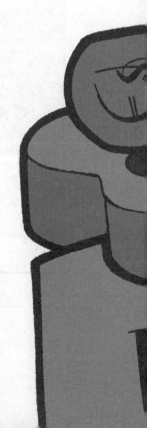

STEP 2

Let's try for a note. Put your first finger down on the fifth fret of the A string. Give the string a pluck and see what you get. If you're not pushing the string down hard enough, it'll buzz and you'll feel it rattle under your finger. However, don't push too hard because that will hurt, and the string will bend causing the pitch to change. All your efforts in the tuning lesson will be wasted!

STEP 3

Now try the sixth fret with your second finger, then the seventh fret with your third finger. Don't forget your little finger gets a turn on the eighth fret.

STEP 4

Do you see that your fingers have lined up over the fifth, sixth, seventh and eighth frets? This is called the 'finger-per-fret' technique. By doing this you should find that you don't have to move your hand up and down the neck, and can play any of those four frets without having to look.

STEP 5

Try this technique on different strings and different frets.

EXERCISE

1. Now we're going to move on a small step from the four plucks per string in the last lesson. This time, have your first finger fret the string you're picking at the fifth fret. On the way back down, move up to the sixth fret.

Start slowly and make sure each note rings out clearly, without any buzzing or rattling. Try the exercise with each fretting finger and get used to the feeling. Experiment on different frets, too. You can pluck all the notes with your thumb or give the I, M and A fingers the G, B and high E strings.

2. The aim of this exercise is to work on the finger-per-fret system. It starts with your first finger on the fifth fret, second finger on the sixth, third finger on the seventh and fourth finger on the eighth. These fingerings are shown above the TAB.

When you get to the high E string, shift all your fingers up one fret by moving your hand along the neck. Your little finger should be on the ninth fret and ready to reverse the pattern to come back down. Keep all your fingers involved, with as little hand movement as possible.

3 & 4. The next examples stay with the finger-per-fret technique but go across the strings in a diagonal pattern. Getting used to these shapes will help when you encounter some tricky chords – they don't get much more stretchy than this! Go nice and slow.

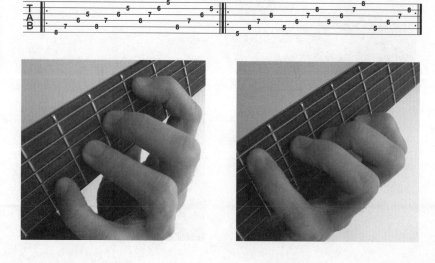

PROBLEM?

If you find your fingers keep rolling over onto their sides, have a look at your elbow position. Move your elbow in or out from your body and you should find it affects the angle of the fingers over the fretboard. A good elbow position should allow you to get your fingertips on the strings and fingers parallel to the frets.

TRACKS 17 & 18

5 & 6. These final exercises have a more melodic sound, rather than a regular finger pattern, and include some open strings. The fingering marked above the music will keep you within the finger-per-fret system.

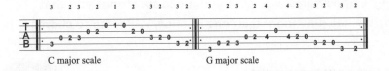

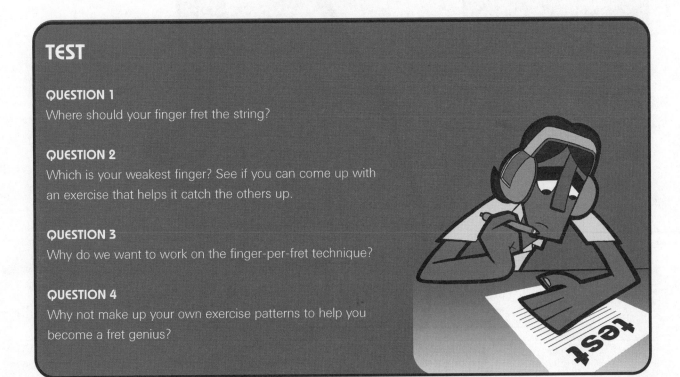

C major scale   G major scale

Use all of these exercises to strengthen fingers and improve co-ordination. The patterns are relatively simple to remember so you can concentrate on the physical side. Don't forget to try playing in time to a metronome or drum beat, like I do on the CD.

TIP

Some of these exercises may be a bit of a stretch until your fingers loosen up and get stronger. If you look at the fretboard you should see that the frets get closer together further up the neck. Try the patterns higher up to start with and then move down as the fingers feel more daring.

TEST

QUESTION 1
Where should your finger fret the string?

QUESTION 2
Which is your weakest finger? See if you can come up with an exercise that helps it catch the others up.

QUESTION 3
Why do we want to work on the finger-per-fret technique?

QUESTION 4
Why not make up your own exercise patterns to help you become a fret genius?

OPEN CHORDS

Hopefully those previous exercises have got your fingers a little better behaved by now! However, all our efforts have been on playing single strings. Well, the guitar has six strings and that means we can play more than one at once. Welcome to chords.

YOUR GOALS

GOAL 1
To learn to read chord charts and diagrams.

GOAL 2
To memorise some open chord shapes.

GOAL 3
To get all the strings ringing clearly.

GOAL 4
To play some fingerstyle over chords.

GOAL 5
To get familiar with the chord sounds.

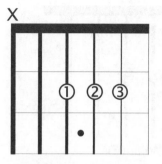

A Major (A)

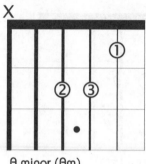

A minor (Am)

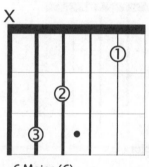

C Major (C)

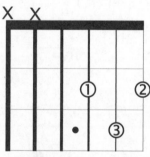

D Major (D)

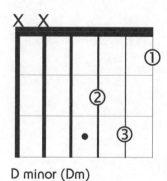

D minor (Dm)

THEORY

We're going to learn some 'open' chords. By this we mean that some of the strings are fretted with the fingers but some are left to ring untouched. A chord is a group of notes played together, and if you pick the right notes it sounds great. The chord shapes in this lesson give us some of the good combinations of notes to play.

To show chords we use chord diagrams that have the six strings from left to right – low E, A, D, G, B, high E. The thick line going across the top is the nut at the end of the neck and then we have the first, second and third fret (indicated with the fret marker).

Basically, put your finger where you see a circle! The number in the circle is the best finger to use so you don't get into a tangle.

Play all the strings with your pick hand unless there's an 'X' above it.

Chords can be powerful things. If you play the right ones, you can make people smile or cry! Major chords tend to give a happy sound. Minor chords have a sad sound. Listen out for this.

LEFT-HANDERS

Chord charts are always drawn for righties. You'll need to get used to reflecting them in your head so the strings and shapes are the other way round, as on your left-handed guitar. The thickness of the string is drawn on these charts to help you find your way. Try angling a small mirror alongside them.

G Major open chord

IN PRACTICE

Let's have a strum and find out what these chords are all about then.

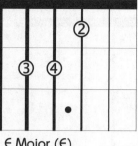

E Major (E)

STEP 1

Choose a chord! You'll probably need to position each finger one by one for the moment, but with practice they'll start to learn the positions for themselves and you'll be able to plonk them all down at once.

STEP 2

Try to bring your fingers in at an angle so it only makes contact with the intended string. Aim to keep your thumb behind the neck for support.

E minor (Em)

STEP 3

Let's have a listen. Picking hand at the ready, hold your thumb or plectrum at the first thick string in the chord and strum down through all of them in one movement.

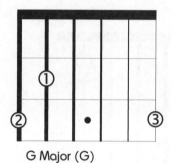

STEP 4

Take all your fingers off and then put them back again. As you learn more chords, practise going from one to another.

G Major (G)

STEP 5

To help memorise the chords, look for patterns within them. For example, join the dots to see that D Major makes a triangle and notice that there's just a small difference between E Major and E Minor.

Each chord has its own challenges. The G and E chords include all six strings, so make sure that they all ring out. D and A Major require your fingers to squeeze into a tight space. With C, A and D chords, be sure not to hit the 'X' strings when strumming the full chord.

EXERCISE

1. This fingerstyle pattern plays the chord as an 'arpeggio'. An arpeggio is when the individual strings are plucked one by one rather than strummed all at once. There is also an alternating bass line where the thumb moves between the D and A strings.

Try to hear how the D string sounds like 'home' and is the correct place for the pattern to stop. This is referred to as the 'root note' of the chord. In all of the chord shapes we've looked at, the root note is the thickest string that we play (without an 'X' above).

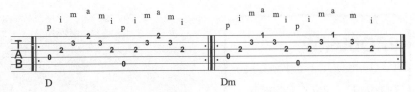

2. These chords all have their root note on the A string, so the patterns start from there. Have a go at this classical-style fingerpicking pattern, marked above the TAB. The thumb plays two strings on the way up and then the index finger plays two on the way back.

3. The next example is written out for E major, a chord shape that includes all six strings. The root note is on the low E string. You can try the same fingerpicking pattern with the other six-string chords – E minor and G major. Here the thumb alternates up and down all three bass strings.

TIP

Acoustic guitar sounds great with big, chiming open chords, but there are only so many shapes we can use. By attaching a capo to a fret you can play all the same shapes higher up the neck. The nut on the chord diagrams is now where the capo is positioned and your fingers take up the chord shape underneath it.

Here are two examples of capos:

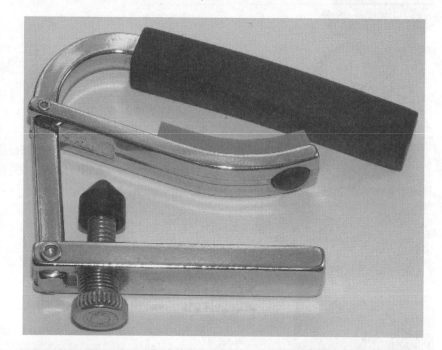

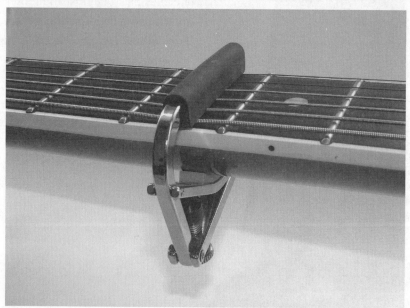

PROBLEM?

If a chord isn't sounding great, pick each string individually and check it's ringing clearly. Don't give up! Getting all the notes to ring properly is quite difficult to start with but you'll gradually get a feel for it. Here's a checklist:

1. Are all your fingers on the correct strings and frets, as in the chord diagram? Make sure that you haven't got two fingers on the same string.

2. Is another finger muting a string by resting against it?

3. Are all your fingers positioned in the fret spaces properly? Check back to the fretting lesson.

4. Make sure you're putting the correct amount of pressure on each of the strings.

TEST

QUESTION 1

What feeling does a minor chord give?

QUESTION 2

Choose some chords and play them one after another to make a chord sequence. Can you can play some well-known songs or make up your own.

QUESTION 3

What does an 'X' mean on a chord diagram?

EAR TRAINING I'll play ten chords. Can you can work out if they are major or minor?

TRACK 22

PICKING

Another approach to plucking and strumming the guitar is to use a plectrum, also known as a 'pick'. The plectrum gives a brighter and more percussive sound, and it's also possible to strum and pick individual strings quicker than with fingerstyle. Complex picking patterns can be tougher, though. Plectrums come in many different colours, but more important are the various thicknesses. See how you get on with a medium thickness – anything too thin and it's like trying to play with a sheet of paper.

YOUR GOALS

GOAL 1
To hold the pick correctly.

GOAL 2
To support your pick hand.

GOAL 3
To pick individual strings accurately and in time.

GOAL 4
To try out different picking directions.

THEORY

Take a look at the photos to see how to grip a pick:

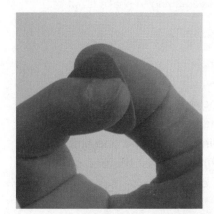
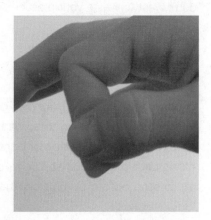

The pointiest part of the pick should come out from the side of your thumb. Grip the pick against the thumb with the side of your first finger curled behind.

We're looking at picking individual strings in this lesson so you need to be accurate. Each string is quite a small target, so try to keep your hand as close to the guitar body as possible. To help, you can anchor your little finger down on the soundboard or rest the heel of your hand on the bridge – make sure it doesn't mute the string you want to play, though.

IN PRACTICE

Give it a go then. Grab the plectrum and be sure not to drop it – you don't want to waste your practice session trying to shake it out of the soundhole!

STEP 1

Choose a string, hold your pick above it and then push through in a downward motion towards the floor. The movement should come from a combination of bending your thumb and first finger along with a bit of wrist. We're aiming for just the one string so try to stop before you hit another one below it. These are called 'downstrokes'.

STEP 2

Now try to pick the string at regular intervals – eg every second a clock ticks. Choose a slow pace that you're comfortable with to start off and only speed up when you're in control and accurate – it'll take a while to get used to the feel.

STEP 3

When you're happy with the downstrokes, try the opposite...an 'upstroke'! Start the pick below the chosen string and move up through it. Again, try this to a regular beat and aim for accuracy rather than speed.

STEP 4

Experiment with different volumes by plucking the strings hard or soft.

STEP 5

Finally, if you're confident with the down and upstrokes separately, try combining the two motions, one after the other – downstroke then upstroke, down, up, down, up, down, up. This is known as 'alternate' picking and will improve your speed.

PROBLEM?

You might find the pick snagging on a string, causing you to lose time or hit other strings when it finally pops out. Firstly, most of the pick is there for you to hold rather than hit the string with – just pick the string with the tip. You can control this by only showing a small amount of the pick from the side of your thumb. Secondly, experiment with the pick angle, going between full-on attack to almost sliding off the string.

TIP

Experiment with your pick-hand position over the guitar body and see how the sound changes. Playing near the bridge gives a bright, fizzy sound. Over the soundhole and close to the neck gives a bassy, mellow sound.

TEST

QUESTION 1

What part of the pick should be hitting the string?

QUESTION 2

How can you make sure you hit the right string without looking?

QUESTION 3

What is the benefit of alternate picking?

QUESTION 4

How does playing with a plectrum differ to fingerstyle?

EXERCISE

Try the following patterns with the plectrum, and also go back to the exercises in the earlier fingerstyle lesson.

1. This exercise should give you a feel for where each string is. Start on the low E and move from one string to the next. Upon reaching the high E, reverse the pattern and head back.

2. In the fingerstyle lesson we looked at plucking each string four times. Here's a variation with a three-notes-per-string pattern.

For each of these exercises try the different picking techniques we've learned – downstrokes, upstrokes and alternate. Give this one a try with the alternate picking. An odd number of picks per string can take a bit of getting used to.

3. Here's an exercise that involves a bit of string-skipping. Try to make sure that you don't hit the string in-between. You can remember the first half of the pattern by thinking 'skip one, back one, skip one, back one', and then reverse it for the trip back.

STRUMMING

Now let's check out some strumming patterns that you can use with the chords we've been looking at.

THEORY

We're going to introduce a bit of traditional music notation here – the blobs and lines you often see pianists playing from. This might not seem too Xtreme but it's actually really good practice and helps to make you aware of what you're playing.

Count out loud '1, 2, 3, 4, 1, 2, 3, 4, etc'. Be sure to count at regular intervals, perhaps every time a clock ticks. Tap your foot with each count so that you're feeling the beat. These are known as quarter notes because there are four of them to each bar. The symbol for a quarter note is the stick with a blob on the end, also known as a 'crotchet'. If you see the squiggly symbol, it still represents a count of one but is a 'rest', so you don't play a note.

Now keep the same count at the same speed but in-between each number say 'and'. So you'll be counting '1 and 2 and 3 and 4 and'. Keep your foot tapping on the numbers and feel the 'and' going in the space. These are eighth notes because there are now eight of them in a bar. An eighth note, also known as a 'quaver', looks similar to the crotchet symbol but it has a little tail hanging off. If there are two of them next to each other, the tails are linked together so that they're easier to spot in a group. There's also an eighth rest that looks a bit like the number 7, so count it but don't play.

 crotchet  rest

It can be good practice giving the count of 1 a bit of extra 'oooomph' to indicate the start of each bar. When there are four quarter notes counted per bar we call this 4/4 time, and you'll see this written at the start of a sheet of music.

♪ quaver   two quavers   ⁊ rest

You can strum the strings with either the plectrum or thumb. We want to get all of the strings ringing with a downward- or upward- brushing motion.

Upstroke

Downstroke

IN PRACTICE

Let's try some of these rhythms on the guitar.

STEP 1

Mute all the strings with your fretting hand by resting the fingers lightly over the fretboard. Don't push the strings down because they'll still make a note. Strum quickly down all the strings. This is a downstroke, just like when we were picking single strings. It is notated with a ⊓ symbol. Try an upstroke. This is notated with a V symbol. With the muting you should just be getting a percussive sound with no ringing strings.

STEP 2

Go back to counting quarter notes – '1, 2, 3, 4'. For each count, strum a downstroke. When you bring your arm up for the next downstroke, make sure that you don't hit the strings. Get a feel for that and keep your foot tapping. Nod your head, too, if you like.

STEP 3

Now we'll go to eighth notes – '1 and 2 and 3 and 4 and'. Keep strumming the downstrokes as you were before but hit the strings on your way back up. These upstrokes become the 'ands' in-between the numbers.

STEP 4

Now leave out the downstrokes so that you're only strumming up on the 'ands'. On the numbers, keep your foot tapping and arm going down (but missing the strings). This is called playing on the 'offbeat'.

STEP 5

We've done all this with your fret hand muting the strings to help concentrate on the strumming. Now try these steps with some of the open chords learned earlier.

TIP

The CD examples all use a click to play along in time to. This is like a simple drum beat that indicates the beats in the bar. Work on your timing by playing along to something that gives you a regular beat – a metronome, drum machine or piece of music with an even tempo.

PROBLEM?

Trouble keeping time? Your strums will stay on the beat if you keep your arm ticking up and down, even when not hitting the strings. Keep a nice smooth strumming motion at all times – no stopping and starting. You don't need the accuracy of single-string picking here so try using more elbow for the motion. It will help to keep your foot tapping on the beats, too.

EXERCISE

I'm going to play all these exercises for you with the E Major open chord. Get used to the rhythms and then experiment with some of the other chords and progressions we've looked at.

Each example has the traditional notation at the top. Below that is the down or upstroke symbol. Underneath those is how to count along.

1. Quarter notes - Downstrokes regularly on the beat.

2. Eighth notes - Downstrokes in the same places as before but with upstrokes in between to make it twice as fast.

3. Offbeat - Eighth notes but only the upstrokes are strummed. Miss the strings on the downstrokes.

4. Now we start to mix them up for more interesting rhythms.

5 & 6. Complicated rhythms now. Keep your arm ticking and watch the count.

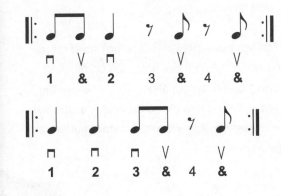

TRACK 26

TRACK 27

TRACK 28

TRACK 29

TRACK 30 & 31

TEST

QUESTION 1
What note value is a crotchet?

QUESTION 2
Which symbol indicates an upstroke?

QUESTION 3
What can you use to practise playing in time?

QUESTION 4
Write out all the eighth notes '1 and 2 and 3 and 4 and'. Scribble out a few beats of your choice, making them rests. Can you play the new rhythm that you've made?

FINGERSTYLE 2

I used to want to be a one-man-band – you know: drums attached to my back and stuff. But I realised that, with a bit of imagination, the guitar can do all that! We're now going to look at some more advanced fingerstyle patterns.

YOUR GOALS

GOAL 1
To pluck with a finger and the thumb simultaneously.

GOAL 2
To run finger patterns over chord changes.

GOAL 3
To play bass lines and melodies...at the same time!

THEORY

When a pianist plays with two hands they can play a bass line with the left and a melody with the right. We're going to do all this with our picking hand. Whooah!

The first fingerstyle lesson was all about playing strings individually. Using similar picking patterns, we will begin plucking more than one string at the same time. Individual musical parts will begin to take shape as one and two string plucks are mixed together.

The additional effect of two strings being played is that they have more emphasis than a single string alone. When these notes fall on different beats in the bar we get an effect called 'syncopation'. This is where the emphasis of a note, or 'accent', falls on an unexpected beat – a little like when we strummed offbeats earlier on. A syncopated rhythm pattern can sound more jumpy and appealing.

IN PRACTICE

OK, let's see if your picking hand can take on a mind of its own!

STEP 1

Have a go at plucking the D and G strings at the same time – the thumb plays the D and the I finger plays the G. The motion of the thumb and finger coming together will feel like you are pinching the strings.

STEP 2

Next, pad away on the D string with your thumb to a regular beat. When you get used to the rhythm, try plucking the G string every two times you play the D. You should be plucking two strings, then one string, two then one, two then one, and so on. This will sound like a simple bass line with a separate melody on the top.

STEP 3

Now, let's reverse the situation. Pad away on the G string with your I finger and play the D string on every other one.

STEP 4

Try both of these patterns with your thumb on different bass strings and using the other fingers.

STEP 5

Instead of playing both strings every two plucks, vary the exercise by playing every three or four.

TIP

There is no shortage of different fingerpicking patterns to invent. You've got six strings to choose from and can play them with any finger or with your thumb. On top of that, you can play strings individually or with others at the same time. See what you can come up with. Don't make them sound too random, though – a catchy pattern will be simple and repetitive rather than overly complex.

EXERCISE

These exercises will be played with some of the open chords that we've learned. Get your fret fingers onto the chord indicated underneath the TAB and then concentrate on the finger picking. You can always work on the finger picking with open strings first, as we did earlier.

1. This example uses a triplet timing, indicated by the 3s above the notation. Count these with a '1 and a, 2 and a, 3 and a, 4 and a' feel. The finger pattern has the thumb playing the bass note on the 1 and 3 counts, which coincides with the A finger on the high E string. We now have the start of melodies and bass working separately.

2. This fingerstyle pattern is quite repetitive. The fret hand goes through some changes to add more to the melody.

3. Take your time to get the picking pattern working here. It includes an alternating bass line for the thumb, too. The second bar on C major requires you to move your third fretting finger between the A and low E string, following the thumb plucks.

Experiment with these fingerpicking patterns over different chord shapes.

PROBLEM?

If the patterns feel like there is too much going on at once, break them down into small chunks. Loop around just two or three of the notes slowly until your fingers get used to it. When you've got a couple of small chunks nailed, stick them together to make the complete pattern. After a few practice sessions the patterns should become automatic, leaving you free to think about chords, and so on.

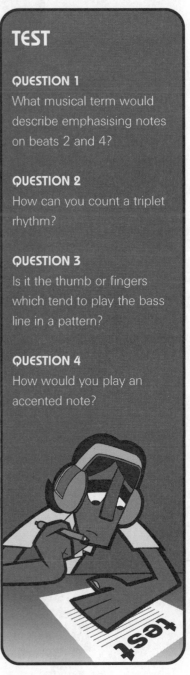

TEST

QUESTION 1

What musical term would describe emphasising notes on beats 2 and 4?

QUESTION 2

How can you count a triplet rhythm?

QUESTION 3

Is it the thumb or fingers which tend to play the bass line in a pattern?

QUESTION 4

How would you play an accented note?

CHORD TECHNIQUES

Yeah, I can see that fingerstyle technique is coming along nicely,
my friend. We must press on: your fretting hand is looking bored!

YOUR GOALS

GOAL 1
To pluck some
doublestops.

GOAL 2
To nail the 'hammer-on'.

GOAL 3
To perfect the 'pull-off'.

GOAL 4
To play around with
fingers in chord shapes.

THEORY

In fingerstyle, we've used the thumb and finger to pluck a bass and melody note at the same time. We're now going to use two adjacent fingers to pluck neighbouring strings in a chord. This is referred to as a 'doublestop'.

The fret hand is also going to learn a new trick. If you whack your fingers down on the fretboard, you'll more than likely hear a note or two. Likewise, when you pull your fingers off the strings, you'll get some sounds.

The 'hammer-on' is the technique of fretting the string quickly and firmly to make a note. The fretted note should sound without the need for a separate pick stroke.

Opposite to the hammer-on is the 'pull-off'. When your finger is already fretting a string, pull it off at an angle so you lightly pluck it and sound the lower note. Again, no need for an extra pick.

These methods are shown on TAB by a tie line linking two or more notes together. So, you pick the first note and then hammer-on or pull-off the note tied to it. You'll usually see an 'H' or 'PO' written above the tie, too. Any strings that are ringing unchanged alongside this will be tied to the same fret number in a bracket.

We'll then apply these techniques within the open chords that we've learned by adding and lifting fingers in and out of the existing shapes. The slight changes in the chord shapes will give new flavours and additional melodies when strumming or finger picking.

TIP

There are a lot more chords out there than the eight open shapes we've looked at. However, most are just small variations in the shapes that we've already learned. You don't need to know the name of a chord to use it! Move a finger or two around in the shapes you already know. Muck about and see what sounds good.

IN PRACTICE

STEP 1

Pluck the open D string. While the note is still ringing, hammer your second finger down quite hard onto the second fret. You should hear the note go up. Keep going between these two notes. The pattern is 'pluck, hammer, pluck, hammer, etc'.

STEP 2

This time, start with your second finger on the second fret. Pick the note and pull the finger away at about 45 degrees from the fretboard, so that the string is plucked and the open note rings out. Repeat the pattern – 'pluck, pull-off, pluck, pull-off, etc'.

STEP 3

Give these two techniques a go with your other fingers and on different frets.

STEP 4

Now try the hammer-on and pull-off techniques within a chord. Fret the C major chord shape and strum it. Try the hammers and pull-offs that we did with the middle finger. Make sure that you keep the first and third finger fretting the C major chord.

STEP 5

Try the doublestop. Squeeze your I and M fingers lightly together and line them up over the G and B strings. Now move both fingers as one to pluck the two strings. Have a go with your M and A fingers, too.

STEP 6

Try doublestopping adjacent strings within the C Major chord. Play the D and G strings with your I and M fingers and run through the hammer-ons and pull-offs.

PROBLEM?

Are your hammer-ons and pull-offs getting lots of unwanted noise or no sound at all? The pull-off is all about the angle at which you pull the finger away. The fingertip needs to get a bit of a grip so that it flicks off the string. If you lift the finger straight up there'll be no sound. If you pull right along the fretboard you'll end up bending the note or hitting neighbouring strings. Find an angle between these and things should sound good. Be accurate with your hammer-ons so as not to catch the wrong strings.

TEST

QUESTION 1

Does a hammer-on make the previous note go up or down?

QUESTION 2

What do we call the technique of plucking two neighbouring strings at the same time?

QUESTION 3

Does a pull-off make the previous note go up or down?

QUESTION 4

Why not have a look back through the previous lessons? When you've got more than one note on a string, try to incorporate the hammer-ons and pull-offs instead of picking everything. See how it sounds and affects your playing.

EXERCISE

These exercises are all adding hammer-ons and pull-offs into the C major chord shape. Have a go at playing the bass notes on the A string with your thumb or a plectrum.

1. This example uses hammer-ons with the middle fret finger and then the index fret finger. Use the fret fingers recommended for C major in the open chord lesson.

2. This example uses the same ideas, but with pull-offs instead.

3. Now we make use of the little fret finger that is normally unused in the C major chord shape. We also mix hammers and pull-offs into the same pattern and alternate between hitting the D and G string.

Try all of these patterns with different chords and see what adjustments you can make to the fingers in the shapes.

MUTING AND PERCUSSION

Awwww, this is our last lesson. Keep up the practising now, you hear? You owe it to the kind trees that made your guitar! In this lesson we're going to look at some muting techniques and see how to get a bit of percussion out of the guitar – after all, that big soundbox is a bit like a drum.

THEORY

Spaces are just as important as notes when it comes to making interesting rhythms. Both hands can be used to control the length of time that a string vibrates. Releasing the finger pressure in a chord will lift the strings off the frets and stop them ringing. The fingers of the fret hand can also deliberately rest lightly over the strings to halt the sound, just as we did in the strumming lesson. Likewise, the pick hand can rest over unwanted strings – perhaps in the middle of a strumming pattern – to create a gap.

I know! You spent the last nine lessons trying to make a noise and now I'm telling you to stop it! However, muting is extremely important and the control it brings will move your playing onto the next level. It may seem like a lot to think about at the moment, but it does become automatic after time and you won't even realise that you're doing it – I nearly forgot to mention it to you actually!

We can also take these muting techniques to create more distinct rhythms. Instead of resting a hand lightly on to the strings, come down quite hard so as to create a percussive sound like banging a drum. Try this out on different areas of the guitar and see what noises you can create. Have a go with different parts of your hand – knuckles or fingernails – to create different effects.

Percussive sounds are marked on the TAB notation with an 'X' symbol instead of a fret number.

YOUR GOALS

GOAL 1
To control how long strings ring out for.

GOAL 2
To create percussive sounds.

GOAL 3
To add extra rhythms to strumming and finger patterns.

GOAL 4
And finally…to experiment! Make up some new stuff!

IN PRACTICE

So, now we'll have a go at taming those wild strings.

STEP 1

Choose an open chord and give it a full, loud strum. You should hear that the strings ring for quite a long time before they finally die out.

STEP 2

Strum that same chord but quickly after it, rest your pick hand down over the strings. They will stop vibrating and be silenced.

STEP 3

Now, try the same again, but this time mute by releasing your fret hand in the chord and resting the fingers lightly on the fretboard.

STEP 4

This time try both techniques again but, rather than resting lightly on to the strings, experiment by hitting down harder. This will make percussive sounds and hence create additional rhythms after the initial strum.

STEP 5

The percussive sound that you get will vary according to where you hit the guitar. Knocking on the soundboard will give a bassy boom. Tapping the side of the body will sound a sharp snap. Hitting the strings down on to the fretboard will give a metallic click.

TIP

With muting it's not just all or nothing, either. Rest your pick hand lightly onto the bridge so that the heel is making slight contact with the strings. Strum or pluck from that position and you'll still get a note, but it'll be dampened. Experiment with the amount of pressure you put onto the strings. This technique is called 'palm muting' and is indicated on music with an 'MU' sign.

EXERCISE

These examples are all based around the E major chord. As usual, give them a try and then experiment with some other chord shapes. Give the various muting and percussive techniques a try where you see the 'X's.

1. Straight quarter beats here. Strum then mute, strum then mute......

2. The previous strums are now doubled to eighth notes with a down and upstroke.

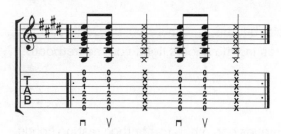

3. In this example try to feel that the mutes are on what would normally be downstroke strums. The strum after each mute is an offbeat upstroke.

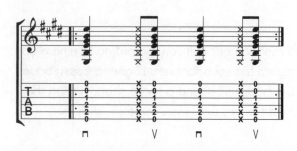

4. Finally, a fingerstyle version. The thumb takes the low E string and all three IMA fingers pluck the G, B and high E string chords at the same time. Watch the rhythm of this one – you should feel your mutes taking the 2 and 4 beats.

TEST

QUESTION 1
How is a percussive mute indicated on a sheet of music?

QUESTION 2
In a five-string chord (eg A minor), how could you stop the low E string from ringing out?

QUESTION 3
How would you play notes marked with the 'MU' sign?

QUESTION 4
Go back to the strumming lesson exercises and swap some strums for percussive mutes. Why not make up your own patterns?

TOP 10 ARTISTS

DAVID GRAY

David Gray grew up in a Welsh fishing village. The first spark of musical interest came when David, aged 13, discovered Bob Dylan in his dad's record collection. Having learned a few chords, he played in some punk-rock bands at school and got into poetry. However, it was during his time at Liverpool University that he realised music was definitely the way to go. After his degree he recorded a demo and handed it about, which eventually resulted in gaining a manager and then a record deal. While very popular in Ireland, thanks to a music TV programme, it did take time for him to get noticed elsewhere. Despite doing plenty of touring with the likes of the Dave Matthews Band and making a few albums, fame took its time. It was three years after the release of Gray's fourth album, *White Ladder*, that he finally entered the UK Top Ten. The album was recorded in a small London flat.

STATISTICS

DATE OF BIRTH
13 June 1968

PLACE OF BIRTH
Manchester, England

INFLUENCES
Bob Dylan, Van Morrison, John Lennon

FIRST HIT
'Babylon' – July 2000

HIGHEST CHART POSITION
'Babylon' – UK # 5 – July 2000

LISTEN TO
'Sail Away'
'Babylon'
'Gutters Full Of Rain'
'Please Forgive Me'

IN THE STYLE OF...

Early Gray tracks were acoustic guitar alone, but David's latest offerings mix the guitar with electronic technology, such as drum machines and samplers. Some songs include simple but effective strums in the background while others have acoustic lead-lines as the main hook.

HOW TO PLAY LIKE DAVID GRAY

Here's a simple lead-line that would sit on top of an electronic-style backing. This part includes the 'slide' technique where you see an 'S' sign. Fret the first note and slide your hand up until the finger reaches the second note; a rigid finger is required to keep the note ringing throughout. This part would be played with a plectrum, although using a thumb and finger will make skipping the B string a little easier.

The next riff is quite spacious, playing tiny sections of the chords C and then G along with a hammer-on and pull-off. Again, a plectrum could be used for a brighter sound.

TRUE STORY!

While touring in the USA, the band stopped off at a café. At this point their bus driver decided to drive off without them, taking all their equipment! One police chase later and the situation was eventually resolved.

SHERYL CROW

Coming from a musical family where both parents performed in orchestras meant that Sheryl Crow was introduced to instruments at an early age. She gained a classical music degree at the University of Missouri, while singing and playing keyboards in a band. However, Crow decided that she didn't want to practise piano every day and turned to guitar, learning songs off records. For a while she earned money by teaching music, playing in cover bands and recording jingles for adverts. In 1986 Sheryl moved to Los Angeles to pursue her own music, while still continuing with session singing. She sang alongside some big-name artists, such as Eric Clapton and Stevie Wonder. Crow's break as a recording artist came from an album that originated from jams at a music club. The single 'All I Wanna Do' made it to the top of the charts and took the album, *Tuesday Night Music Club,* with it. Various awards followed, along with further albums, a cover of the Guns N' Roses track, 'Sweet Child O' Mine' and the title theme to the James Bond film, *Tomorrow Never Dies*.

STATISTICS

DATE OF BIRTH
11 February 1962

PLACE OF BIRTH
Kennett, Missouri, USA

INFLUENCES
Bob Dylan, Fleetwood Mac, John Hiatt, Joni Mitchell

FIRST HIT
'All I Wanna Do' – September 1994

HIGHEST CHART POSITION
'All I Wanna Do' – US # 2 – September 1994

LISTEN TO
'A Change Would Do You Good'
'Home'
'Strong Enough'
'The First Cut Is The Deepest'

IN THE STYLE OF...

Sheryl Crow's good-time, radio-friendly rock songs give country-style acoustic parts and catchy chord-based riffs. She mainly uses a pick with a style taken from Bob Dylan's influence.

HOW TO PLAY LIKE SHERYL CROW

Here's a fingerstyle pattern that combines bass notes, chords and a melody into each bar. Take note that this example uses the 6/8 time signature – this means that instead of counting to four, you count to six. It gives the piece a jolly, jumpy feel. Check out the rhythm on the CD.

The next riff is what you might normally play on an electric guitar, but it works just as well as a rocky acoustic part. Looking at the first small chord, the best way to finger it is to flatten your first finger across all three strings on the fifth fret, forming a 'barre'. Your second and third fingers can then take up position on the seventh fret strings. Using a plectrum, strum it with the alternate 'down, up, down, up' pattern and you'll find that the strokes marked on the music fall into place. Also, attempt to mute the other strings with your fretting hand to allow the strumming hand to play more freely.

FRANCIS HEALY

Fran Healy is the frontman singer/guitarist for British band Travis. His musical ability started to show at the age of six, when he won a traditional Scottish song competition at school. Glasgow-based Travis formed in 1990. After finishing at art school, they began to work hard on songs and getting the band heard. To concentrate on song writing, Fran was once sent to a flat for six days with nothing but £20, a Beatles album and a four-track recorder. He returned with hit songs that they recorded as a small demo. Moving to London in 1996, Travis signed their first record deal and began touring with the likes of Oasis, which set the stage for their first album, *Good Feeling*. It wasn't until their fifth single, 'Writing To Reach You', gained radio attention that they received full recognition, inspiring further acoustic rock bands, such as Coldplay, to make their move.

STATISTICS

DATE OF BIRTH
23 July 1973

PLACE OF BIRTH
Stafford, England

GENRE
Pop/rock

INFLUENCES
Joni Mitchell, The Beatles, Max Martin, Neil Young

FIRST HIT
'U16 Girls' – April 1997

HIGHEST CHART POSITION
'Sing' – UK # 3 – June 2001

LISTEN TO
'Writing To Reach You'
'Why Does It Always Rain On Me?'
'Sing'
'Turn'

IN THE STYLE OF...

The Travis songwriter sets the scene for their songs with acoustic strums over stirring chord sequences. Moving bass lines are as complex as it gets, leaving space for sing-along vocal melodies and catchy riffs from the electric guitar.

HOW TO PLAY LIKE FRANCIS HEALY

Here is a typical Travis strumming pattern that should be played with a plectrum for a bright sound. You need to feel the 'swing' in the rhythm indicated at the start of the notation – the upstrokes come slightly later than with a normal eighth note. If you count in triplets – '1 and a, 2 and a, 3 and a, 4 and a' – you will strum downstrokes on the numbers and upstrokes on the 'a'. Listen to the CD example to hear exactly how it should sound. The chords start with a happy D major and move to a sadder-sounding A minor. The last two bars bring the bass line up to raise the mood and start again.

TRACK 50 & 51

The next example could be played with a plectrum or with fingers – both will be a good exercise. If fingerpicking, remember to keep your thumb handling the three bass strings. Also, experiment between letting each note ring throughout and keeping them short by resting your hand lightly on the strings near the bridge. You might find Travis playing this sort of pattern on a banjo.

TRACK 52 & 53

Fran makes plenty of use of the capo, so give these examples a try further up the neck.

ANI DIFRANCO

The soloist Angela Marie DiFranco is a folk singer/guitarist with a punk direction. At the age of nine, Ani's parents took her to buy a guitar. It was in the shop that they met a folk singer who fixed up her first gig, performing some Beatles covers. Ani had always been into poetry and began writing songs at 14 after a brief departure from music to study ballet. The regular gigging life kicked off at 15, with songs being written at such a rate that she had over 100 under her belt before the age of 20. Relentless touring inevitably led to fans and record company interest, but she ignored their offers and founded her own business, Righteous Babe Records. Ani has now released more than 20 self-produced albums.

STATISTICS

DATE OF BIRTH
23 September 1970

PLACE OF BIRTH
Buffalo, New York, USA

GENRE
Folk rock

INFLUENCES
The Beatles, Woodie Guthrie, Pete Seeger, Suzanne Vega

FIRST HIT
'Dilate' – May 1996

HIGHEST CHART POSITION
'Little Plastic Castle' – US #22 – March 1998

LISTEN TO
'Gravel'
'Pulse'
'Tip Toe'
'Both Hands'

IN THE STYLE OF...

Ani Difranco's versatile guitar playing often sounds like it's coming from more than one guitar. Her riffs go from soft to angry in the space of a split-second. The aggressive picking-hand technique makes you feel sorry for the strings, giving not only melodies but percussion too. Difranco songs can also vary from standard tunings, including DADGAd and EADGAd.

HOW TO PLAY LIKE ANI DIFRANCO

First up is a grabbing fingerstyle example. With your thumb on the bass note, hook your three fingers under the other strings in the chord and then pluck all at the same time. A lot of Ani's riffs are very 'staccato' (the notes she plays are very short). These are indicated by the 'CO' signs in the music, which stands for 'cut off'. As soon as you pluck the strings, get your fingers back in position for the next pluck, thus muting the strings quickly. The ⟨ symbols indicate a crescendo – start plucking the notes quietly and gradually get louder.

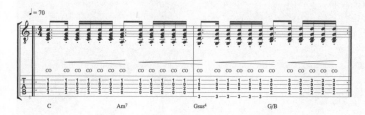

The second example should be strummed with a plectrum for maximum attack. The 'X' symbols indicate a percussive mute, which is done by landing the entire pick hand onto the strings in a downstroke. This example finishes off with a natural harmonic. Do this by lightly resting a finger directly over the fret wire indicated (but don't press down) – you should get a really high note.

DAMIEN RICE

Damien Rice brings us guitar and vocals with moving orchestral accompaniments. Along with spending his childhood fishing and painting, he taught himself to play guitar. Damien initially had more of a lead-guitar approach, playing electric in a band at school. His first taste of recording was with the indie-rock band Juniper, which did quite well in Ireland. However, the direction set by the record company was not what Rice wanted. He left the band in 1999 to go travelling and busking around Europe. The trip brought Damien back to acoustic guitar, and when he returned to Dublin a year later he was ready for more. A demo was recorded and sent to his second cousin, David Arnold, a producer and film soundtrack composer. This led to the album *O*, an instant hit in Ireland in 2001, and later in the UK.

STATISTICS

DATE OF BIRTH
7 December 1973

PLACE OF BIRTH
Dublin, Eire

GENRE
Folk

INFLUENCES
Leonard Cohen, Radiohead, Nina Simone, Jacques Brel

FIRST HIT
'The Blower's Daughter' – September 2001

HIGHEST CHART POSITION
'Cannonball' – UK # 32 – November 2003

LISTEN TO

'The Blower's Daughter'
'Volcano'
'Eskimo'
'Cannonball'

IN THE STYLE OF...

Damien creates strong and magical folk melodies on his debut album, *O*. The songs feature a lot of mellow strumming with the thumb, some fingerstyle and also a bit of picking with the plectrum. This mixture of picking styles gives a wide range of sounds and dynamics.

HOW TO PLAY LIKE DAMIEN RICE

Both of these examples would be strummed with down and upstrokes from the thumb. As with the Sheryl Crow example, this first piece is another to use the 6/8 time signature. As usual, pay attention to the strumming notation to help with timing and keep things flowing naturally. A hammer-on is used in both the G and C chord shapes, while the final bars slide the open C chord shape up two frets to make a tasty D chord. Watch out for the first two bars being repeated three times before moving onto the final part.

With the second example keep your thumb ticking up and down to 16th notes, which can be counted as '1 e and a, 2 e and a, 3 e and a, 4 e and a'. Aim roughly for the strings marked out but don't worry about being too accurate, just as long as the strums emphasise the melody within the part. You might find it useful for your spare pick-hand fingers to anchor down on the guitar body and rest against the high E string to mute it.

Take these parts and experiment with a capo for higher voicings.

NEIL YOUNG

Neil Young set out performing as a solo folk artist. However, over time his songwriting has taken him from folk to rock, country and even grunge, with some electronic effects thrown in. He began playing music at high school, being a member of a number of bands. In the mid-'60s, after getting some folk gigs in clubs, Young moved to Los Angeles and made his first hits with the band Buffalo Springfield. Since then, the albums and tours have kept coming, with Neil changing between solo and band line-ups as it suits his style. More recent work, including an album with Pearl Jam in 1995 and an appearance for MTV Unplugged, has ensured his music is always winning new fans, young and old. He has established himself as one of the most influential songwriters, alongside the likes of Bob Dylan.

STATISTICS

DATE OF BIRTH
12 November 1945

PLACE OF BIRTH
Toronto, Ontario, Canada

GENRE
Rock

INFLUENCES
Bob Dylan, The Rolling Stones, Bert Jansch, Jimi Hendrix

FIRST HIT
'For What It's Worth' (with Buffalo Springfield) – February 1967

HIGHEST CHART POSITION
'Heart Of Gold' – US # 1 – February 1972

LISTEN TO
'Sugar Mountain'
'Heart Of Gold'
'My My, Hey Hey'
'Ambulance Blues'

IN THE STYLE OF...

Over the last 30 years, Neil has worked hard in a variety of musical styles. While also being partial to some heavy electric guitar, his acoustic guitar playing features mainly in the folk genre. He demonstrates some complex fingerstyle with bluesy melodies in the chords, along with plectrum-strumming patterns that contain interesting muted rhythms and examples of melodies in the bass.

HOW TO PLAY LIKE NEIL YOUNG

This plectrum-strummed example should be muted slightly by resting the heel of your picking hand on the strings just above the bridge – this is indicated in the notation with the 'MU' sign. The first and third bars chug along with downstrokes. Try slightly bouncing your picking hand on and off the strings as you strum to mute and release.

The second exercise contains a fast hammer-on within the open D shape chord. This riff is then varied by moving the bass underneath to form a chord sequence. The last bar has a bass line that brings it back to the start.

TRACKS 61 & 62

CD

TRACKS 63 & 64

CD

SUPERSTAR TIP!

Neil isn't interested in mastering scales and technique. His outlook is that you can play any note you like, how you like. After learning a few basic chords and riffs, you can experiment and adapt them to create your own sounds.

TRUE STORY!

One of Neil's bands, Buffalo Springfield, came together on 6 April 1966. It was all down to a chance meeting of the members while they were stuck in a Los Angeles traffic jam!

NICK DRAKE

During Nick Drake's short lifetime his gentle folk music went almost unnoticed, but slowly the word is getting around. He was brought up in the village of Tamworth-In-Arden, England, and started guitar at the age of 16. Four years later, in 1967, he made some recordings at his parent's home that impressed Joe Boyd, a producer who worked in folk-rock. Nick was offered a contract, and the first album, *Five Leaves Left*, was released in 1969. However, Drake was very shy and didn't like to perform live, which made it very difficult for people to find out about his music. Nick also began to suffer from depression. Sadly, it was only another two albums and a few spare tracks that were recorded before he died on 26 November 1974. However, the nature of Drake's music is such that once a person hears it, they never forget it, and tell others. This slow spread of followers is increasing all the time, and he is now viewed as a hugely influential artist. A fourth album of unreleased material was produced after he died.

STATISTICS

DATE OF BIRTH
19 June 1948

PLACE OF BIRTH
Rangoon, Burma

GENRE
Folk

INFLUENCES
Bert Jansch, John Renbourn, Van Morrison, Tim Buckley

FIRST HIT
No singles released

HIGHEST CHART POSITION
N/A

SUPERSTAR TIP!

Nick's songs use various non-standard tunings, away from the usual EADGBe. It is thought that he would begin writing a song in a standard tuning and make adjustments as he heard different things, retuning a string to make fingerings easier and new notes possible. Adjusting your tuning will change all the normal chord shapes and scales that we learn, so make sure you're confident with the basics before making things even more complicated!

LISTEN TO

'Time Has Told Me'
'River Man'
'Northern Sky'
'Pink Moon'

IN THE STYLE OF...

Nick's distinct and original sound is sometimes haunting and mysterious, but also relaxing. Soft vocals are accompanied by complex finger-picking patterns, made even more interesting by the varied guitar tunings.

HOW TO PLAY LIKE NICK DRAKE

Example one is a fingerstyle pattern with a country-style edge to it. The second section is a trickier version of the same pattern, which adds a bit more melody. Notice that the thumb just keeps quarter notes padding away on the A string while the fingers either play at the same time or in the gaps. Practise these patterns slowly in small chunks and then piece them together when confident.

TRACKS 65 & 66

A more mysterious piece follows, making use of the triplet swing feel from the Fran Healy example. Another catch is a strange 5/4 time signature where each bar contains a count of five, not four. Listen to the CD to get a feel for what's what. Use your thumb for the bass notes and all three IMA fingers to pluck the chords above. The second bar contains an F chord – try holding the bass note on the first fret with the thumb of your fret hand.

TRACKS 67 & 68

TRUE STORY!

One of Drake's most outstanding songs 'Know' is actually one of the most simple you could come across. It consists of Nick humming over a short four-note repeated riff.

JONI MITCHELL

Born Roberta Joan Anderson in Alberta, Canada, Joni took the surname Mitchell from her first marriage. Learning to play the guitar from a book by Pete Seeger, Joni was absorbed in music and painting from an early age. At college she began performing folk songs. The year 1968 saw the release of Joni's first record and her song writing began to get attention from other artists wanting to perform her tracks. Her music began to earn a strong following as the styles travelled from folk to pop, jazz and world music. Up to this day, Joni has released more than 20 albums and worked with the likes of Peter Gabriel, Jaco Pastorius and Tom Petty. In 2002, Mitchell came close to retiring until a friend introduced her to a synthesizer guitar. It opened up a whole new range of sounds, simplifying her various alternative tunings, and was the source of inspiration she needed to continue.

STATISTICS

DATE OF BIRTH
7 November 1943

PLACE OF BIRTH
Alberta, Canada

GENRE
Rock

INFLUENCES
Bob Dylan, Joan Baez

FIRST HIT
'You Turn Me On (I'm A Radio)' - US # 25 – February 1973

HIGHEST CHART POSITION
'Help Me' – US # 7 – February 1974

LISTEN TO

'Big Yellow Taxi'
'Chelsea Morning'
'You Turn Me On (I'm A Radio)'
'Both Sides Now'

IN THE STYLE OF...

Joni's songwriting skills and excellent vocals are supported by
bright, exciting guitar playing. Over time, her many songs have
been estimated to make use of more than 50 different tunings!
This is one reason why she had a break from touring in the '80s
as it was getting a little difficult to handle. Her sound often
incorporates pedal tones – where a consistent note is present
in the range of chords.

HOW TO PLAY LIKE JONI MITCHELL

This first example demonstrates the use of open strings with a small
sliding chord shape. Get used to the fingerstyle pattern in the first bar
(as it is the same throughout) and then work with the chords in the later
sections. Notice how the open strings combined with different chord
positions can make it sound like the picking pattern is changing.

The next piece would be strummed with a plectrum, but feel free to
experiment with fingers. Watch for the down and upstrokes indicated,
and keep the arm ticking on 16th notes, as seen in the Damien Rice
example. The rhythm can be helped along by squeezing your fret
fingers in the chord only when it is to be heard. Cut the chord short
after each strum by releasing the pressure in your hand.

BOB DYLAN

Bob Dylan is widely regarded as one of the greatest songwriters, with many musicians playing his compositions. He learned to play guitar, piano and harmonica as a child, and formed a rock 'n' roll band at high school. While studying art at the University of Minnesota, he began performing folk songs. Regular gigs got him spotted and signed in 1961, and a string of albums were to follow at regular intervals through to the '90s. Dylan's second album, *The Freewheelin'*, broke the mould of artists only performing other writers' songs: this record contained all his own material. It paved the way for other artists to follow, writing and recording their own music, as is commonplace today. Over the next few decades his styles went from folk, blues, R&B, rock 'n' roll, country and then back round again, while changing from solo acoustic artist to full electric band. These shifts have often upset fans who were into his previous style, but they soon caught up!

STATISTICS

DATE OF BIRTH
24 May 1941

PLACE OF BIRTH
Duluth, Minnesota

GENRE
Folk rock

INFLUENCES
Hank Williams, Woody Guthrie, Odetta, Jesse Fuller, Little Richard

FIRST HIT
'Times They Are A-Changin''
– March 1965

HIGHEST CHART POSITION
'Like A Rolling Stone' –
US # 2 – August 1965

LISTEN TO

'Lay Lady Lay'
'Maggie's Farm'
'Knockin' On Heaven's Door'
'Like A Rolling Stone'

IN THE STYLE OF...

The large number of people who refer to Bob Dylan as their biggest influence just goes to show how important he is to popular music. His distinctive singing voice sits on top of perfectly crafted chord sequences, with most of his melodic work being drawn from chord shapes, be it in rhythm parts or solos.

HOW TO PLAY LIKE BOB DYLAN

Here we have a picked exercise that fits over the chord sequence G, Bm, A, C#m. It'll be good practice to try this with fingerstyle, too.

TRACKS 73 & 74

Next up is an example of using dynamics in your strumming. The start of this part has the 'mp' sign, which stands for mezzo piano. This means to strum 'medium soft'. Increase the volume towards the end of the sequence, indicated by the ⟨ sign leading up to the 'f', which stands for forte and means 'loud'. Use a constant ticking down–up pattern on the eighth notes with open chords. The small > signs beneath the note heads indicate accents, so emphasise these strums.

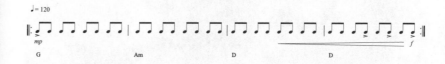

TRACKS 75 & 76

SUPERSTAR TIP!

Bob's genius is sometimes the simplicity of his guitar playing, making the most of simple chords and only a few choice notes for melodies. Work really hard on perfecting the basic stuff and you'll have people queuing up to play your songs, just like Dylan does. Check out 'Knockin' On Heaven's Door', performed by Guns N' Roses, and 'All Along The Watchtower', performed by Jimi Hendrix.

TRUE STORY!

Bob Dylan was born Robert Allen Zimmerman. He changed his name when he started gigging, taking his surname from the poet Dylan Thomas.

CHET ATKINS

Born Chester Burton Atkins, he was later to become known as 'Mister Guitar'. Chet's first instrument was the fiddle but he quickly turned to the guitar at the age of nine. After high school, Chet entered the world of session work by playing for radio shows. This exposure led to a call from RCA studios, Nashville, who he joined in 1949. The long list of albums began to be released in 1953. These demonstrated an incredible fingerpicking ability and knack for arranging traditional tunes for solo guitar. Continuing to work as a session player, he climbed the ladder from Nashville consultant to manager and then vice president of country music. It was Chet's work in these areas that made him responsible for moving country music into the charts and creating the 'Nashville sound'. He worked with the likes of Elvis Presley, Jerry Reed, Paul McCartney, Mark Knopfler and Tommy Emmanuelle.

STATISTICS

DATE OF BIRTH
20 June 1924

PLACE OF BIRTH
Luttrell, Tennessee, USA

GENRE
Country

INFLUENCES
Les Paul, Django Reinhardt, Merle Travis

FIRST HIT
'Mr Sandman' – 1955

HIGHEST CHART POSITION
'Yakety Axe' – US Top 5 –1965

LISTEN TO
'Mr Sandman'
'Big Foot'
'Black Mountain Rag'
'Sweet Georgia Brown'

IN THE STYLE OF...

Chet Atkins is usually the first name to pop up when fingerstyle is mentioned. His use of a thumb-pick and fingers to produce bass, melody and harmony all at the same time meant he didn't really need a band. He was even known to mic up his foot taps, just to make sure the drummer was out of a job, too!

HOW TO PLAY LIKE CHET ATKINS

Here's a country fingerstyle example that has your thumb alternating between two strings on the bass line. Doublestops fit into the gaps and should be plucked with your I and M fingers. Cut these notes short by returning your fingers straight away for the next pluck.

TRACKS 77 & 78

Chet is famous for his mellow tone and chiming solo runs. The next line is a solo run that would fit over a G chord (the last bar in the previous example perhaps). The inclusion of the open strings gives this a bright sound and helps to keep the notes ringing out as you descend the scale. It's all topped off with a natural harmonic at the end, as seen in the Ani Difranco example.

TRACK 79

GLOSSARY

8VA
The notes are played an octave higher than indicated.

ACCENT
To emphasise or stress a note.

ALTERNATE PICKING
To pick repeatedly with a downstroke followed by an upstroke, rather than all in the same direction.

ARPEGGIO
The notes of a chord played individually one after another instead of all at once.

BARRE
When the underside of a finger frets across a number of strings.

CAPO
A device for effectively creating a new nut, higher up the neck.

CHORD
A combination of three or more notes played at the same time.

CRESCENDO
To get gradually louder.

CROTCHET
The notation symbol to indicate a quarter note.

CUT OFF (CO)
To play a note and quickly cut it short by muting. Also known as Staccato.

DOUBLESTOP
Two notes played on neighbouring strings.

FLAT (♭)
A note that is lower in pitch.

FORTE (F)
Loud.

HAMMER-ON (H)
Making the string sound by hitting it onto the fretboard.

METRONOME
A device that indicates a regular time interval with a click sound or flashing light.

MEZZO PIANO (MP)
Medium soft.

MUTE (MU)
To reduce the vibration of the strings by resting the hand or fingers over them.

NATURAL HARMONIC (NH)
Created by picking a string while lightly touching the suggested fret (5th, 7th or 12th is good).

NC
'No Chord' – to indicate that a chord shouldn't be played over a section of the music.

OPEN
Strings that are played without being fretted.

PIMA
The convention used to label picking fingers.

PULL-OFF (PO)
Making the string sound by quickly pulling the finger away from the fretboard with a light pluck.

QUAVER
The notation symbol to indicate an eighth note.

REST
The notation symbol to indicate a period of silence.

ROOT
The note that a chord or scale is built from.

SCALE
A sequence of notes in a specific order.

SEMIQUAVER
The notation symbol to indicate a 16th note.

SHARP (♯)
A note that is raised in pitch.

SLIDE (S)
To fret a note and slide the finger up or down the neck, maintaining the sound throughout.

STACCATO
See 'Cut Off'.

SYNCOPATION

To accent a note on an unexpected beat.

TEMPO

The speed of the beats in the music, measured in BPM (Beats Per Minute).

TIE

The line linking two notes together. Only the first note in the tie is picked, eg a hammer-on. Also used to indicate when a note should continue ringing from one bar to the next.

TIME SIGNATURE

The sign at the start of a piece of music indicating the number and type of beats in a bar.

ANSWERS TO TEST QUESTIONS

LESSON 1
1. Right-handers pick with the right hand. Left-handers the left.
2. Different picking methods give different sounds and make certain picking and strumming patterns possible.
3. Stop playing, stretch out and take a rest.
4. Playing the guitar in a different position will feel strange and require more practice.

LESSON 2
1. Every Angry Dog Growls Before Eating.
2. The B string.
3. 'B to C' and 'E to F'.
Ear training CD:
a. In tune
b. Sharp
c. Flat
d. Sharp
e. Flat
f. Flat
g. In tune
h. In tune
i. Flat
j. Sharp

LESSON 3
1. The B string.
2. The ring/third finger.
3. Keep a part of your picking hand in contact with the guitar. Anchor your little finger down on the soundboard or rest the heel of your hand on the bridge.

LESSON 4
1. Just before the fret wire.
2. Usually the third or fourth finger. Make an exercise that concentrates on using that finger to fret the strings.
3. It is very efficient. The hand can stay still and you can find any of the frets under the fingers without looking.

LESSON 5
1. Sad
3. Don't play the string that the 'X' is above.
Ear training CD:
a. Major
b. Minor
c. Minor
d. Major
e. Major
f. Major
g. Minor
h. Major
i. Minor
j. Minor

LESSON 6
1. The pointed end.
2. Anchor your little finger down on the soundboard or rest the heel of your hand on the bridge.
3. It is very efficient and improves speed.
4. It gives a brighter and more percussive sound and enables you to pick individual strings quickly.

LESSON 7
1. A quarter note. One count.
2. V
3. A metronome, drum machine or piece of music with an even tempo.

LESSON 8
1. Syncopation.
2. '1 and a 2 and a 3 and a 4 and a'.
3. Thumb (P).
4. Emphasise the note (eg pluck the string harder for more volume).

LESSON 9
1. Up.
2. Doublestop.
3. Down.

LESSON 10
1. With the 'X' sign.
2. By muting it with a spare fretting-hand finger or by bringing the thumb round the side of the neck.
3. Lightly mute them by resting the heel of the picking hand over the strings.